£3

anarchist pocketbooks

From riot to insurrection

Analysis for an anarchist perspective against post industrial capitalism

ALFREDO M. BONANNO

Introduction by
JEAN WEIR

ELEPHANT EDITIONS

This pocketbook published in 1988 by
Elephant Editions, B.M. Elephant, London
WC1N3XX

Cover illustration and design by Clifford Harper

Translated by Jean Weir

Printed in Catania by
Alfa Grafica Sgroi
Via S. Maria della Catena 87 — Catania (Italy)
January 1988

CONTENTS

INTRODUCTION

There can be little doubt left anywhere on the planet that a fundamental change is taking place in the organisation of production. This change is most obvious and most felt in the centres of advanced capitalism, but the logic of information technology and decentralised production now reaches what were once remote periferal areas, drawing them into an artificial communitarianism whose only real element is exploitation.

In the "western world" the traditional worker, cornerstone of the authoritarian revolutionary thesis, and still a principle element in many anarchist ones, is being tossed out of the grey graveyards of docks, factories and mines, into the coloured graveyards of home-videos, brightly lit job-centres, community centres, multi-ethnic creches, etc, in the muraled ghettos.

As unemployment is coming to be accepted as a perspective of non-employment, capital continues to refine its instruments and direct investment to areas more befitting to its perennial need for expansion. Production of consumer goods is now realised by an inter-continental team of robots, small self-exploiting industries, and domestic labour, in many cases that of children.

The trade unions are at an ebb, and the parties of the left are creeping further to the right as areas for wage claims and social reform are disappearing from the electoral map. What is emerging instead are wide areas of progressive "democratic dissent" in political, social and religious terms: pacifism, ecologism, vegetarianism, mysticism, etc. This "dissenting consensus" sees its most extreme expression in the proposals of "delegitimisation" and "deregulation" by a privileged intellectual strata that reasons exclusively in terms of its own rights.

An ideal society, it might seem, from capital's point of view, with social peace as one of its prime objectives today; or so it would be, this "self-managed" capitalist utopia, were it not for the threat coming from outside this landscaped garden. From the ghetto areas, no longer confined to the Brixton, Toxteth model, but which take many forms: the mining village of the north, the gigantic, gloomy labyrinths of council estates in urban complexes, many of them already no-go areas to police and other forces of repression, and other ever widening areas which until recently housed secure well-paid skilled and white collar workers, are on their way to becoming new ghettos. The ghettos of the future, however, will not necessarily be geographically circumscribed, as the hotbeds of unrest are farmed out to bleak and manageable dimensions, but will be culturally defined, through their lack of means of communication with the rest of capitalist society.

The presence of these ever widening ghettos and the message that is crying out from them is the main flaw in the new capitalist perspective. There are no mediators. There is no space for the reformist politicians of the past, just as there is none for the essentially reformist revolutionaries of the old wokerist structures, real or imaginary. The cry is a violent one that asks for nothing. The mini riots or explosions that are now common occurances, especially in this country, do not have rational demands to make. They are not the means to an end like the bread riots of the past. They have become something in themselves an irrational thrusting out, often striking easily identifiable targets of repression (police stations, vehicles, schools, government offices, etc), but not necessarily so. Violence in the football stadiums cannot be excluded from this logic.

Anarchists, since the first major riots—Bristol, Brixton, Toxteth, Broadwater Farm—have seen these events in a positive light, often joining in and contributing a number of extra bricks in the direction of police lines. Anarchist journals exalt these moments of mass insurgence, yet at the same time (the same papers) provide organisational proposals which, if they might have been valid at the beginning of the century or in the 'thirties, certainly bear no resemblance to the needs of the present day. The best the most updated ones can offer, using the riots as their point of reference, is to create a specific movement of anarchists with the aim of instilling some revolutionary morality into these patently amoral events. Once again the poverty of our analytical capacity comes to bear.

Up until now, when anarchists have had need of, some theoretical content in their publications, they have either resorted to personal opinion, or given a summary of some of the Marxist analyses, critically, but often underlining that there are some points in Marxism that are relevant to anarchist ideas. This gives a "serious" content to a periodical, shows that we are not against theoretical discussions, but leaves the field for anarchist action barren. Without analysis, even at the most basic, rudimentary level, we cannot hope to be in touch with reality. Intuition is not enough. We cannot hope to act, pushing contradictions towards a revolutionary outlet, by simply responding to events as they arise, no matter how violent these events may be.

The Marxist analyses are now nothing but obsolete relics of the dark ages of industrialism. What must be done is to develop our own theses, using as a foundation the wealth of our anarchist methodological heritage. The great strength of anarchism is the fact that it does not rely on one fundamental analysis anchored in time. The living part of anarchism is as alive today as it was four decades ago, or a century ago. What we need to do is to develop instruments that take what is relevant from the past, uniting it with what is required to make it relevant to the present. This can only be done if we have a clear idea what that reality is. Not what we would like it to be, but what it is, of what is emerging as the real battleground of exploitation today, for battleground it is, even though the dead and wounded have a different aspect to those of yesterday, and the just response of the exploited takes new, less explicit forms. The need to act becomes more pressing as the ghettos become encapsulated and segregated from the mainstream language and communication of the privileged.

The analyses we are presenting here opens a door in that direction, gives a glimpse of what is happening around and stimulous to develop further investigation and to seek to formulate new forms of anarchist intervention that relate to this reality, trying to push it towards our goal of social revolution.

The first text was originally written and presented as the theme of an anarchist conference in Milan in October 1985, held by the comrades of the Italian anarchist bimonthly *Anarchismo*. The second part is a spoken contribution by the same comrade. This explains the concise nature of the text. The author has in fact dedicated many more pages to the insurrectional thesis, work that he has developed through his active involvement in struggles in Italy over the past two decades.

Jean Weir

FOR AN ANALYSIS OF A PERIOD OF CHANGE

FROM POST-INDUSTRIAL ILLUSIONS TO POST-REVOLUTIONARY ONES

Changes in society

In the evolution of social contradictions over the past few years, certain tendencies have become so pronounced that they can now be considered as real changes.

The structure of domination has shifted from straightforward arbitrary rule to a relationship based on adjustment and compromise. This has led to a considerable increase in demand for services compared to such traditional demands as for durable consumer goods. The results have been an increase in those aspects of production based on information technology, the robotisation of the productive sector, and the pre-eminence of the services sector (commerce, tourism, transport, credit, insurance, public administration, etc) over industry and agriculture.

This does not mean that the industrial sector has disappeared or become insignificant; only that it will employ fewer and fewer workers while levels of production remain the same, or even improve. The same is true of agriculture, which will be greatly affected by the processes of industrialisation, and distinguishable from industry in statistical rather than social terms.

This situation is developing more as a "transition", not something that is cut and dried, but as a trend. There is no distinct separation between the industrial and post-industrial periods. The phase we are passing through is clearly one of surpassing the obsolete institutions which are being restructured; but it has not yet reached the closure of all factories and the establishment of a reign of computerised production.

The tendency to break up units of production and the demand for small self-exploiting nucleii within a centralised productive project will predominate in the next few years. But within the industrial sector this will be accompanied by such slow adjustments, using traditional means, as are expedient to the cautious strategies of capital.

This argument relates more to the British and Italian situations which remain far behind their Japanese and American models.

Islands of lost men

Torn from the factories in a slow and perhaps irreversible process, yesterday's workers are being thrown into a highly competitive atmosphere. The

14

aim is to increase productive capacity, the only consumable product according to the computerised logic of the centres of production. The atomised (and even more deadly) conflicts within capital itself will extinguish the alternative, revolutionary struggle, with the intention of exacerbating class differences and rendering them unbridgeable.

The most important gains for the inhabitants of the productive "islands", their seemingly greater "freedom", the flexible working hours, the qualitative changes (always within the competitive logic of the market as directed by the order-giving centres) reinforce the belief that they have reached the promised land: the reign of happiness and well-being. Ever increased profits and ever more exacerbated "creativity".

These islands of death are surrounded by ideological and physical barriers, to force those who have no place on them back into a tempestuous sea where no one survives.

So the problem revealing itself is precisely that of the e x c l u d e d.

Two reservoirs of the revolution

The e x c l u d e d and the i n c l u d e d.

The first are those who will remain marginalised. Expelled from the productive process and penalised for their incapacity to insert themselves into the new competitive logic of capital, they are often not prepared to accept the minimum levels of survival assigned to them by State assistance (increasingly seen as a relic of the past in a situation that tends to extoll the virtues of the "self-made man"). These will not just be the social strata condemned to this role through their ethnic origin —today, for example, the West Indians in British society, catalysts of the recent riots in that country—but with the development of the social change we are talking about, social strata which in the past were lulled by secure salaries and now find themselves in a situation of rapid and radical change will also participate. Even the residual supports that these social strata benefit from (early pensions, unemployment benefit, various kinds of social security, etc) will not make them accept a situation of growing discrimination. And let us not forget that the degree of consumerism of these expelled social strata cannot be compared to that of the ethnic groups who have never been brought into the sphere of salaried security. This will surely lead to explosions of "social illbeing" of a different kind, and it will be up to revolutionaries to unite these with the more elementary outbreaks of rebellion.

Then there are the i n c l u d e d, those who will remain suffocating on the islands of privilege. Here the argument threatens to become more complicated and can only be clearly situated if one is prepared to give credit to man and his real need for freedom. Almost certainly it is the "homecomers" from this sector who will be among the most merciless executants of the attack on capital in its new form. We are going towards a period of bloody clashes and very harsh repression. Social peace, dreamt of on one side and feared by the other, remains the most inaccessable myth of this new capitalist utopia, heir to the "pacific" logic of liberalism which dusted the drawing room while it butchered in the kitchen, giving welfare at home and massacring in the colonies.

The new opportunities for small, miserable, loathsome daily liberties will be paid for by profound, cruel and systematic discrimination against vast social strata. Sooner or later this will lead to the growth of a consciousness of exploitation inside the privileged strata, which cannot fail to cause rebellions, even if only limited to the best among them. Finally, it should be said that there is no longer a strong ideological support for the new capitalist perspective such as existed in the past, capable of giving support to the exploiters and, more important still, to the intermediate layers of cadres. Wellbeing for the sake of it is not enough, especially for the many groups of people who, in the more or less recent past, have experienced, or simply read about, liberatory utopias, revolutionary dreams and the attempts, however limited, at insurrectional projects.

The latter will lose no time in reaching the

others. Not all the i n c l u d e d, will live blissfully in the artificial happiness of capital. Many of them will realise that the misery of one part of society poisons the appearance of wellbeing of the rest, and turns freedom (within the barbed wire fences) into a virtual prison.

State precautions

Over the past few years the industrial project has also been modified by the fusion of State controls and methods linked with the political interest in controlling consensus.

Looking at things from the technical side, one can see how the organisation of production is being transformed. Production no longer has to take place in one single location, (the factory), but is more and more spread over a whole territory, even at considerable distances. This allows industrial projects to develop that take account of a better, more balanced distribution of productive centres within a territory, eradicating some of the aspects of social disorder which have existed in the past such as ghetto areas and industrial super-concentions, areas of high pollution and systematic destruction of the eco-systems. Capital is now looking forward to an ecological future, opening its arms to the great hotchpotch of environmentalists and becoming a champion of the safeguarding of natural resources, so making the construction seem possible of cities of the future with a "human face", socialist or not.

The real motivation driving the capitalist project towards distant lands resembling the utopias of yesteryear, is very simple and in no way philanthropic: it is the need to reduce class discontent to a minimum, smoothing the edges off any effective confrontation through a sugar-coated progressive development based on blind faith in the technology of the future.

It is obvious that the most attractive proposals will be made to the i n c l u d e d, to try as far as possible to avoid defections, which will be the real thorn in the side of tomorrow's capitalists. The individual subjects, if they come from within the sphere of the production process, who turn their goals in a revolutionary direction, will have real weapons to put at the disposal of the revolution against the rule of exploitation.

So far the utopian hope of governing the world through "good" technology has shown itself to be impossible, because it has never taken into account the problem of the physical dimension to be assigned to the ghetto of the e x c l u d e d. They could be recycled into the garden-project in an ungenerous mixture of happiness and sacrifice, but only up to a point.

Tension and repeated explosions of rage will put the fanciful utopia of the exploiters into serious difficulty.

The end of irrational competition

It has long been evident. Competition and monopolism were threatening to draw the productive structures into a series of recurrent "crises". Crises of production in most cases. For the old capitalist mentality it was essential to achieve so-called "economies of scale", and this was only possible by working with ever larger volumes of production in order to spread the fixed costs as far as possible. This led to a standardisation of production: the accumulation of productive units in particular locations, distributed haphazardly with a colonising logic (for example the classical Sicilian "cathedrals in the desert": isolated industrial areas, petrol refineries, etc that were to serve as points of aggregation); the uniformity of products; the division of capital and labour, etc.

The first adjustments to this came about through massive State intervention. The State's presence has opened up various opportunities. It is no longer a passive spectator, simply capital's "cashier", but has become an active operator, "banker" and entrepreneur.

In essence, these adjustments have meant the diminution of use value, and an increase in the production of exchange value in the interests of maintaining s o c i a l   p e a c e.

In bringing to an end its most competitive period, capital has found a partial solution to its problems. The State has lent a hand with the aim of completely transforming economic production into the production of social peace. This utopian project is clearly unreachable. Sooner or later the machine will shatter.

The new productive process—which has often been defined p o s t - i n d u s t r i a l —makes low production costs possible even for small quantities of goods; can obtain considerable modifications in production with only modest capital injections; makes hitherto unseen changes to products possible. This opens up undreamt of horizons of "freedom" to the middle classes, to the productive cadres, and within the golden isolation of the managerial classes. But this is rather like the freedom of the castle for those Teutonic knights of the nazi kind. Encircled by the mansion walls, armed to the teeth, only the peace of the graveyard reigns within.

None of the makers of the ideologies of post-industrial capitalism have asked themselves what to do about the danger that will come from the other side of the walls.

The riots of the future will become ever more bloody and terrible. Even more so when we know how to transform them into mass insurrections.

Consciousness and ghettoisation

It will not be unemployment as such which

negatively defines those to be excluded from the castle of Teutonic knights, but principally the lack of real access to information.

The new model of production will of necessity reduce the availability of information. This is only partly due to the computerisation of society. It is one of the basic conditions of the new domination and as such has been developing for at least twenty years, finding its climax in a mass schooling which is already devoid of any concrete operative content.

Just as the coming of machines caused a reduction in the capacity for self-determination during the industrial revolution, trooping the mass of workers into factories, destroying peasant culture and giving capital a work force who were practically incapable of "understanding" the contents of the new mechanised world that was beginning to loom up; so now the computer revolution, grafted to the process of adjustment of capitalist contradictions by the State, is about to deliver the factory proletariat into the hands of a new kind of machinery that is armed with a language that will be comprehensible to only a privileged few. The remainder will be chased back and obliged to share the sort of the ghetto.

The old knowledge, even that filtered from the intellectuals through the deforming mirror of ideology, will be coded in a machine language and rendered compatible with the new needs. This will be one of the historic occasions for discovering, among other things, the scarcity of real content in the ideological jibberish that has been administered to us over the past two centuries.

Capital will tend to abandon everything not immediately translatable into this new generalised language. Traditional educative processes will become devalued and diminish in content, unveiling their real (and selective) substance as merchandise.

In the place of language new canons of behaviour will be supplied, formed from fairly precise rules, and mainly developed from the old processes of democratisation and assembly, which capital has learned to control perfectly. This will be doubly useful as it will also give the e x c l u d e d the impression that they are "participating" in public affairs.

The computerised society of tomorrow could even have clean seas and an "almost" perfect safeguarding of the limited resources of the environment, but it will be a jungle of prohibitions and rules, of nightmare in the form of deep personal decisions about participating in the common good. Deprived of a language of common reference, the ghettoised will no longer be able to read between the lines of the messages of power, and will end up having no other outlet than spontaneous riot, irrational and destructive, an end in itself.

The collaboration of those members of the i n -

c l u d e d, disgusted with the artificial freedom of capital, who become revolutionary carriers of an albeit small part of this technology which they have managed to snatch from capital, will not be enough to build a bridge or supply a language on which to base knowledge and accurate counter-information.

The organised work of future insurrections must solve this problem, must build—perhaps starting from scratch—the basic terms of a communication that is about to be closed off; and which, precisely in the moment of closure, could give life, through spontaneous and uncontrolled reactions, to such manifestations of violence as to make past experiences pale into insignificance.

Generalised impoverishment

One should not see the new ghetto as the shanty town of the past, a patchwork of refuse forced on to suffering and deprivation. The new ghetto, codified by the rules of the new language, will be the passive beneficiary of the technology of the future. It will also be allowed to possess the rudimentary manual skills required to permit the functioning of objects which, rather than satisfy needs, are in themselves a colossal need.

These skills will be quite sufficient for the impoverished quality of life in the ghetto.

It will even be possible to produce objects of

considerable complexity at a reasonable cost, and advertise them with that aura of exclusiveness which traps the purchaser, now a prey to capital's projects. Moreover, with the new productive conditions we will no longer have repetitions of the same object in series, or change and development in technology only with considerable difficulty and cost. Instead there will be flexible, articulated processes that are interchangeable. It will be possible to put the new forms of control into use at low cost, to influence demand by guiding it and thus create the essential conditions for the production of social peace.

Such apparent simplification of life, both for i n c l u d e d and e x c l u d e d, such technological "freedom" has led sociologists and economists —as the good people they have always been—to let go and sketch the outlines of an interclassist society capable of living "well" without re-awakening the monsters of the class struggle, communism or anarchy.

The decline of interest in the unions and the removal of any reformist significance they might have had in the past—having become mere transmission belts for the bosses' orders—has come to be seen as the proof of the end of the class struggle and the coming of the post-industrial society. This does not make sense for a variety of reasons which we shall see further on. Trade unionism of any kind has lost its reformist significance, not because the class struggle is over, but because the conditions of the clash have changed profoundly.

Basically, we are faced with the continuation of contradictions which are greater than ever and remain unresolved.

Two phases

To be schematic, two phases can be identified.

In the industrial period capitalist competition and production based on manufacturing, prevailed. The most significant economic sector was the secondary one (manufacturing), which used the energy produced as the transformative resource, and financial capital as the strategic resource. The technology of this period was essentially mechanical and the producer who stood out most was the worker. The methodology used in the projects was empirical, based on experiment, while the organisation of the productive process as a whole was based on unlimited growth.

In the post-industrial period which we are approaching, but have not completely entered, the State prevails over capitalist competition and imposes its systems of maintaining consensus and production, with the essential aim of promoting social peace. The elaboration of data and the transformation of services will take the place of the technical mode of manufacturing. The predominant economic sectors become the tertiary (services), the quaternary (specialised finance), the quinary (research, leisure, education, public administration). The main transformative resource is information which is composed of a complex system of transmission of data, while the strategic resource is provided by the knowledge that is slowly taking the place of financial capital. Technology is abandoning its mechanical component and focussing itself on its intellectual component. The typical element employed by this new technology is no longer the worker but the technician, the professional, the scientist. The method used in the project is based on abstract theory, not experiment as it once was, while the organisation of the productive process is based on the coding of theoretical knowledge.

The sunset of the worker's leading role

Directing our attention to the productive industrial phase, marxism considered the contribution of the working class to be fundamental to the revolutionary solution of social contradictions. This resulted in the strategies of the workers' movement being greatly conditioned by the objective of conquering power.

Hegelian ambiguity, nourished by Marx, lay at the heart of this reasoning: that the dialectical opposition between proletariat and bourgeoisie could be exacerbated by reinforcing the proletariat indirectly through the reinforcement of capital

27

and the State. So each victory by repression was seen as the anti-chamber of the future victory of the proletariat. The whole was set in a progressive vision—typically illuminist—of the possibility of building the "spirit" in a world of matter.

With a few undoubtedly interesting modifications, this old conception of the class struggle still persists today, at least in some of the nightmarish dreams that arise occasionally from the old projects of glory and conquest. A serious analysis has never been made of this purely imaginary conception.

There is only more or less unanimous agreement that workers have been displaced from their central position. First, timidly, in the sense of a move out of the factory into the whole social terrain. Then, more decisively, in the sense of a progressive substitution of the secondary manufacturing sector by the tertiary services sector.

The sunset of some of the anarchists' illusions

Anarchists have also had illusions and these have also faded. Strictly speaking, while these illusions were never about the central role of workers, they often saw the world of work as being of fundamental importance, giving precedence to industry over the primary (agricultural) sector. It was anarcho-syndicalism that fuelled these illusions.

Even in recent times there has been much enthusiasm for the CNT's rise from the ashes, particularly from those who seem to be the most radical entrepreneurs of the new "roads" of reformist anarchism today.

The main concept of this worker centrality (different from that of the marxists, but less so than is commonly believed), was the shadow of the Party.

For a long time the anarchist movement has acted as an organisation of synthesis, that is, like a party.

Not the whole of the anarchist movement, but certainly its organised forms.

Let us take the Italian FAI* for example. To this day it is an organisation of synthesis. It is based on a programme, its periodical Congresses are the central focus for its activity, and it looks to reality outside from the point of view of a "connecting" centre, ie, as being the synthesis between the reality outside the movement (revolutionary reality), and that within the specific anarchist movement.

Of course, some comrades would object that these remarks are too general, but they cannot deny that the mentality which sustains the relation of synthesis that a specific anarchist organisation establishes with the reality outside the movement, is one that is very close to the "party" mentality.

Good intentions are not enough.

*
Federazione anarchica italiana

Well, this mentality has faded. Not only among younger comrades who want an open and i n - f o r m a l relationship with the revolutionary movement, but, more important, it has faded in social reality itself.

If industrial conditions of production made the syndicalist struggle reasonable, as it did the marxist methods and those of the libertarian organisations of synthesis, today, in a post-industrial perspective, in a reality that has changed profoundly, the only possible strategy for anarchists is an informal one. By this we mean groups of comrades who come together with precise objectives, on the basis of affinity, and contribute to creating mass structures which set themselves intermediate aims, while constructing the minimal conditions for transforming situations of simple riot into those of insurrection.

The party of marxism is dead. That of the anarchists too. When I read criticisms such as those made recently by the social ecologists who speak of the death of anarchism, I realise it is a question of language, as well as of lack of ability to examine problems inside the anarchist movement, a limitation, moreover, that is pointed out by these comrades themselves. What is dead for them—and also for me—is the anarchism that thought it could be the organisational point of reference for the next revolution, that saw itself as a structure of synthesis aimed at generating the multiple forms of human creativity directed at breaking up State structures of consensus and repression. What is dead is the static anarchism of the traditional organisations, based on claiming better conditions, and having quantitive goals. The idea that social revolution is something that must necessarily result from our struggles has proved to be unfounded. It might, but then again it might not.

Determinism is dead, and the blind law of cause and effect with it. The revolutionary means we employ, including insurrection, do not necessarily lead to social revolution. The causal model so dear to the positivists of the last century does not in reality exist.

The revolution becomes possible precisely for that reason.

Speed and multiplicity

The reduction of time in data-transmission means the acceleration of programmed decision-making. If this time is reduced to zero (as happens in electronic "real time"), programmed decisions are not only accelerated but are also transformed. They become something different.

By modifying projects, elements of productive investments are also modified, transferring themselves from traditional capital (mainly financial) to the capital of the future (mainly intellectual).

The management of the different is one of the fundamental elements of real time.

By perfecting the relationship between politics and economy, putting an end to the contradictions produced by competition, by organising consensus and, more importantly, by programming all this in a perspective of real time, the power structure cuts off a large part of society: the part of the e x c l u-d e d .

The greatly increased speed of productive operations will more than anything else give rise to a cultural and linguistic modification. Here lies the greatest danger for the ghettoised.

End of reformism, end of the party

The party is based on the reformist hypothesis. This requires a community of language, if not of interest. That happened with parties and also with trade unions. Community of language translated itself into a fictitious class opposition that was characterised by a request for improvements on the one hand, and resistance to conceding them on the other.

To ask for something requires a language "in common" with whoever has what we are asking for.

Now the global repressive project is aimed at breaking up this community. Not with the walls of special prisons, ghettoes, satellite cities or big industrial centres; but, on the contrary, by decentralising production, improving services, applying ecological principles to production, all with the most absolute segregation of the excluded.

And this segragation will be obtained by progressively depriving them of the language that they possessed in common with the rest of society.

There will be nothing left to ask.

The dumb excluded

In an era that could still be defined as industrial, consensus was based on the possibility of participating in the benefits of production. In an era where capital's capacity to change is practically infinite, the capital/State duo will require a language of its own, separate from that of the e x - c l u d e d in order to best achieve its new perspective.

The inaccessability of the dominant language will become a far more effective means of segregation than the traditional confines of the ghetto. The increasing difficulty in attaining the dominant language will gradually make it become absolutely "other". From that moment it will disappear from the desires of the e x c l u d e d and remain ignored by them. From that moment on the i n c l u d e d will be "other" for the e x c l u d e d and vice versa.

This process of exclusion is essential to the repressive project. Fundamental concepts of the past, such as solidarity, communism, revolution, anarchy, based their validity on the common recognition of the concept of equality. But for the inhabitants of the castle of Teutonic knights the e x c l u d e d will not be men, but simply things, objects to be bought or sold in the same way as the slaves were for our predecessors.

We do not feel equality towards the dog, because it limits itself to barking, it does not "speak" our language. We can be fond of it, but necessarily feel it to be "other", and we do not spare much thought for its kind, at least not at the level of all dogs, preferring to attach ourselves to the dog that provides us with its obedience, affection, or its fierceness towards our enemies.

A similar process will take place in relation to all those who do not share our language. Here we must not confuse language with "tongue". Our progressive and revolutionary tradition has taught us that all men are equal over and above differences of mother tongue. We are speaking here of a possible repressive development that would deprive the e x c l u d e d of the very possibility of communicating with the i n c l u d e d. By greatly reducing the utility of the written word, and gradually replacing books and newspapers with images, colours and music, for example, the power structure of tomorrow could construct a language aimed at the e x c l u d e d alone. They, in turn, would be able to create different, even creative, means of linguistic reproduction, but always with their own codes and quite cut out of any contact with the code of the i n c l u d e d, therefore from any possibility of understanding the world of the latter. And it is a short step from incomprehension to disinterest and mental closure.

Reformism is therefore in its death throes. It will no longer be possible to make claims, because no one will know what to ask for from a world that has ceased to interest us or to tell us anything comprehensible.

Cut off from the language of the i n c l u d e d, the e x c l u d e d will also be cut off from their new technology. Perhaps they will live in a better, more desirable world, with less danger of apocalyptic conflicts, and eventually, less economically caused tension. But there will be an increase in irrational tension.

From the most peripheral areas of the planet, where in spite of "real time" the project of exploitation will always meet obstacles of an ethnic or geographical nature, to the more central areas where class divisions are more rigid, economically based conflict will give way to conflictuality of an irrational nature.

In their projects of control the i n c l u d e d are aiming at general consensus by reducing the economic difficulties of the e x c l u d e d. They could supply them with a prefabricated language to allow a partial and sclerotised use of some of the dominant technology. They could also allow them a better quality of life. But they will not be able to prevent the outbursts of irrational violence that arise from feeling useless, from boredom and from the deadly atmosphere of the ghetto.

For example in Britain, always a step ahead in the development of capital's repressive projects, it is already possible to see the beginning of this tendency. The State certainly does not guarantee survival, there is an incredible amount of poverty and unemployment, but the riots that regularly break out there are started by young people—especially West Indian—who know they are definitively cut off from a world that is already strange to them, from which they can borrow a few objects or ways of doing things, but where they are already beginning to feel "other".

From irrational riot to conscious insurrection

The mass movements that make such an impression on some of our comrades today because of their dangerous and—in their opinion—uselessness, are signs of the direction that the struggles of tomorrow will take.

Even now many young people are no longer able to evaluate the situation in which they find themselves. Deprived of that minimum of culture that school once provided, bombarded by messages containing aimless gratuitous violence, they are pushed in a thousand ways towards impetuous, irrational and spontaneous rebellion, and deprived of the "political" objectives that past generations believed they could see with such clarity.

The "sites" and expressions of these collective explosions vary a great deal. The occasions also. In each case, however, they can be traced to an intolerance of the society of death managed by the capital/State partnership.

It is pointless to fear those manifestations because of the traditional ideas we have of revolutionary action within mass movements.

It is not a question of being afraid but of passing to action right away before it is too late.

A great deal of material is now available on techniques of conscious insurrection—to which I myself have made a contribution—from which comrades may realise the superficiality and inconclusiveness of certain preconceived ideas that tend to confuse instead of clarify.

Briefly, we reaffirm that the insurrectionary method can only be applied by informal anarchist organisations. These must be capable of establishing, and participating in the functioning of, base structures (mass organisations) whose clear aim is to attack and destroy the objectives set by power, by applying the principles of self-management, permanent struggle and direct action.

SPOKEN CONTRIBUTION TO ANARCHIST CONFERENCE HELD IN MILAN ON OCTOBER 13 1985, ON THE THEME "ANARCHISM AND INSURRECTIONAL PROJECT"

In organising a conference like this there's a strange contradiction between its formal aspect—such a beautiful hall (though that's a matter of taste), finding ourselves like this, with me up here and so many comrades down there, some I know well, others less so—and the substantial aspect of discussing a problem, or rather a project, that foresees the destruction of all this. It's like someone wanting to do two things at once.

This is the contradiction of life itself. We are obliged to use the instruments of the ruling class for a project that is subversive and destructive. We face a real situation that is quite terrible, and in our heads we have a project of dreams.

Anarchists have many projects. They are usually very creative, but at the centre of this creativity lies a destructive project that isn't just a dream, a nightmarish dream, but is something based upon, and verified in, the social process around us.

In reality we must presume that this society, lacerated and divided by oppositions and contradictions, is moving, if not exactly towards one final destructive explosion, at least towards a series of small destructive eruptions.

In his nightmares this is what the man in the street imagines insurrection to be. People armed, burning cars, buildings destroyed, babies crying, mothers looking for lost children. The great problem is that on this subject the thinking of many anarchists is also not very clear.

I have often spoken to comrades about the problems of insurrectional and revolutionary struggle, and I realise that the same models exist in their minds. What is often visualised are the barricades of the eighteenth century, the Paris Commune, or scenes from the French Revolution.

Certainly, insurrection involves this, but not this alone. The insurrectional and revolutionary process is this but also something more. We are here today precisely to try and understand this a little better. Let's leave the external aspects of the problem, look one another in the eye, and try thinking about this for a few minutes.

Let us get rid of the idea of insurrection as barricades and instead see in what way the instrument "insurrection" can be observed in reality today, that is, in a reality which is undergoing a rapid and profound transformation.

Today we are not in 1871, nor 1830, nor '48. Nor are we at the end of the eighteenth century. We are in a situation where industrial production is in transformation, a situation usually described by a phrase, which for convenience we can also use, a "post-industrial" situation.

Some comrades who have reached this analysis, and who have thought about the profound changes that are taking place in the productive situation today, have come to the conclusion that certain old revolutionary models are no longer valid, so that it is necessary to find new ways which not only replace these models, but substantially deny them, and they propose new forms of intervention.

Put this way things seem more logical, in fact, fascinating. Why should one endorse a cheque that expired 100 years ago? Who would ever think that the models of revolutionary intervention of 150 years ago, or even 200 years ago, could still be valid? Of course we are all easily impressed by new roads and new ways of intervening in reality, by creativity and by the new directions that the objective situation today puts at our disposal. But wait a moment.

We don't intend to use literary quotations here. But someone once said that the capacity of the revolutionary was to grasp as much of the future as possible with what still exists from the past. To marry the knife of our ancestors with the computer of the future. How does this come about?

Not because we are nostalgic for a world where man went to attack his enemy with a knife between his teeth, but quite the contrary, because we consider the revolutionary instruments of the past to be still valid today. Not because of any decision by a minority who take them up and establish this validity demagogically without caring what people might think; but because the capacity of the people to find simple means readily at hand, to support any explosion of reactions to repression, represents the traditional strength of every popular uprising.

Let's try to take things in order. There was always something that did not work right with the capitalist project. All those who have ever had anything to do with economic or political analysis have been forced to admit this. Capital's utopia contains something technically mistaken, that is, it wants to do three things that contradict one other: to assure the wellbeing of a minority, exploit the majority to the limits of survival, and prevent insurgence by the latter in the name of their rights.

In the history of capitalism various solutions have been found, but there have been critical moments when capital has been obliged to find other solutions. The American crisis between the two wars, to give a fairly recent example: a great crisis of capitalist over-production, a tragic moment linked to other marginal problems that capital had had to face. How did it manage to solve the problem? By entering the phase of mass consumerism, in other words by proposing a project of integration and participation that led—after the experience of the second world war—to an extension of consumerism and thus to an increase in production.

But why did that crisis raise such serious problems for capital? Because until recently capital could not bring about production without recourse to huge investment. Let us underline the word "until yesterday", when capital had to introduce what are known as e c o n o m i e s o f s c a l e, and invest considerable amounts of financial capital in order to realise necessary changes in production. If a new type of domestic appliance or a new model of car was required, investment was in the order of hundreds of millions.

This situation confronted capital with the spectre of overproduction and with the need to co-opt more and more of the popular strata into massive acquisition. Anyone can see that this could not go on for ever, for sooner or later the game had to end in social violence. In fact the myriad of interventions by capital and State in their attempts to co-opt turned out to be short-lived. Many will remember how ten or fifteen years ago the economists called for economic planning and the possibility of finding work for everyone. That all went up in smoke. The fact is that they were then—note the past tense—moving towards situations of increasing tension. The next stage proposed by capital was to have State structures intervene in capitalist management, that is, to transform the State from simple armed custodian of capital's interests into a productive element within capitalism itself. In other words from cashier to banker. In this way, a considerable transformation took place, because the contradictions of economic competition that were beginning to show themselves to be fatal could be overcome by the introduction of consumerism into the strata of the proletariat.

Today we are faced with a different situation, and I ask you to reflect on the importance of this, comrades, because it is precisely the new perspective that is now opening up in the face of repression and capital's new techniques for maintaining consensus, that makes a new revolutionary project possible.

What has changed? What is it that characterises post industrial reality?

What I am about to describe must be understood as a "line of development". It is not a question of capital suddenly deciding to engineer a transformation from the decision making centres of the productive process, and doing so in a very short space of time. Such a project would be fantastic, unreal. In fact, something like a half-way solution is taking place.

We must bear this in mind when speaking of post-industrial reality because we don't want—as has already happened—some comrade to say: wait a moment, I come from the most backward part of

Sicily where still today labourers are taken on every Sunday by foremen who appear in the piazza offering them work at 5000 Lire per day*. Certainly, this happens, and worse. But the revolutionary must bear those things in mind and at the same time be aware of the most advanced points of reference in the capitalist project. Because, if we were only to take account of the most backward situations we would not be revolutionaries, but simply recuperators and reformists capable only of pushing the power structure towards perfecting the capitalist project.

To return to our theme, what is it that distinguishes post-industrial from industrial reality? Industrial reality was obviously based on capital, on the concept that at the centre of production there was investment, and that that investment had to be considerable. Today, with new programming techniques, a change in the aim of capitalist production is quite simple. It is merely a question of changing computer programmes.

Let's examine this question carefully. Two robots in an industry can take the place of 100 workers. Once, the whole production line had to be changed in order to alter production. The 100 workers were not able to grasp the new productive project instantly. Today the line is modified through one important element alone. A simple

*

about two pounds and fifty pence

45

operation in computer programming can change the robots of today into those of tomorrow at low cost. From the productive point of view capital's capacity is no longer based on the resources of financial capital, on investment in other words, but is essentially based on intellectual capital, on the enormous accumulation of productive capacity that is being realised in the field of computer science, the new development in technology that allows such changes.

Capital no longer needs to rely on the traditional worker as an element in carrying out production. This element becomes secondary in that the principal factor in production becomes intellectual capital's capacity for change. So capital no longer needs to make huge investments or to store considerable stocks in order to regain its initial outlay. It does not need to put pressure on the market and can distribute productive units over wide areas, so avoiding the great industrial centres of the past. It can prevent pollution. We will be able to have clean seas, clean air, better distribution of resources. Think, comrades, reflect on how much of the material that has been supplied to the capitalists by ecologists will be used against us in the future. What a lot of work has been done for the benefit of capital's future plans. We will probably see industry spread over whole territories without the great centres like Gela, Syracuse, Genova, Milan, etc. These will cease to exist.

Computer programming in some skyscraper in Milan, for example, will put production into effect in Melbourne, Detroit or anywhere else. What will this make possible? On the one hand, capital will be able to create a better world, one that is qualitatively different, a better life. But who for? That is the problem. Certainly not for everybody. If capital was really capable of achieving this qualitatively better world for everyone, then we could all go home—we would all be supporters of the capitalist ideology. The fact is that it can only be realised for some, and that this privileged strata will become more restricted in the future than it was in the past. The privileged of the future will find themselves in a similar situation to the Teutonic knights of mediaeval times, supporting an ideology aimed at founding a minority of "equals" —of "equally" privileged—inside the castle, surrounded by walls and by the poor, who will obviously try continually to get inside.

Now this group of privileged will not just be the big capitalists, but a social strata that extends down to the upper middle cadres. A very broad strata, even if it is restricted when compared to the great number of the exploited. However, let's not forget that we are speaking of a project that exists only in tendency.

This strata can be defined as the "included", composed of those who will close themselves inside this castle. Do you think they will surround themselves with walls, barbed wire, armies, guards or police? I don't think so.

Because the prison walls, the ghetto, the dormitory suburb and repression as a whole: police and torture—all of those things that are quite visible today, where comrades and proletarians all over the world continue to die under torture—well, all this could undergo considerable changes in the next few years. It is important to realise that five or ten years today corresponds to 100 years not long ago. The capitalist project is travelling at such speed that it has a geometric progression unequalled to anything that has happened before. The kind of change that took place between the beginning of the 60's and 1968 takes place in only a few months today.

So what will the privileged try to do? They will try to cut the e x c l u d e d off from the i n - c l u d e d. Cut off in what way? By cutting off communication.

This is a central concept of the repression of the future, a concept which, in my opinion, should be examined as deeply as possible. To c u t o f f c o m m u n i c a t i o n means two things. To construct a r e d u c e d language that is modest and has an absolutely elementary code to supply to the excluded so that they can use the computer terminals. Something extremely simple that will keep them quiet. And to provide the included, on the other hand, with a language of "the included", so that their world will go towards that utopia of privilege and capital that is sought more or less everywhere. That will be the real wall: the lack of a common language. This will be the real prison wall, one that is not easily scaled.

This problem presents various interesting aspects. Above all there is the situation of the included themselves. Let us not forget that in this world of privilege there will be people who in the past have had a wide revolutionary-ideological experience, and they may not enjoy their situation of privilege tomorrow, feeling themselves asphyxiated inside the Teutonic castle. These will be the first thorn in the side of the capitalist project. The class h o m e c o m e r s , that is, those who abandon their class. Who were the h o m e c o m - e r s of the class of yesterday? I, myself, once belonged to the class of the privileged. I abandoned it to become "a comrade among comrades", from privileged of yesterday to revolutionary of today. But what have I brought with me? I have brought my Humanist culture, my ideological culture. I can only give you words. But the homecomer of tomorrow, the revolutionary who abandons tomorrow's privileged class, will bring technology with him, because one of the characteristics of tomorrow's capitalist project and one of the essential conditions for it to remain standing, will be a distribution of knowledge that is no longer pyramidal but horizontal. Capital will need to distribute knowledge in a more reasonable and equal way—but always within the class of the included. Therefore the deserters of tomorrow will bring with them a considerable number of usable elements from a revolutionary point of view.

And the excluded? Will they continue to keep quiet? In fact, what will they be able to ask for once communication has been cut off? To ask for something, it is necessary to know what to ask for. I cannot have an idea based on suffering and the lack of something of whose existence I know nothing, which means absolutely nothing to me and which does not stimulate my desires. The severing of a common language will make the reformism of yesterday—the piecemeal demand for better conditions and the reduction of repression and exploitation—completely outdated. Reformism was based on the common language that existed between exploited and exploiter. If the languages are different, nothing more can be asked for. Nothing interests me about something I do not understand, which I know nothing about. So, the realisation of the capitalist project of the future—of this post-industrial project as it is commonly imagined—will essentially be based on keeping the exploited quiet. It will give them a code of behaviour based on very simple elements so as to allow them to use the telephone, television, computer terminals, and all the other objects that will satisfy the basic, primary, tertiary and other needs of the excluded and at the same time ensure that they are kept under control. This will be a painless rather than a bloody procedure. Torture will come to an end. No more bloodstains on the wall. That will stop—up to a certain point, of course. There will be situations where it will continue. But, in general, a cloak of silence will fall over the excluded.

However, there is one flaw in all this. Rebellion in man is not tied to need alone, to being aware of the lack of something and struggling against it. If you think about it this is a purely illuminist concept which was later developed by English philosophical ideology—Bentham and co.—who spoke from a Utilitarian perspective. For the past 150 years our ideological propaganda has been based on these rational foundations, asking why it is that we lack something, and why it is right that we should have something because we are all equal; but, comrades, what they are going to cut along with language is the concept of equality, humanity, fraternity. The included of tomorrow will not feel himself humanly and fraternally similar to the excluded but will see him as something o t h e r. The excluded of tomorrow will be outside the Teutonic castle and will not see the included as his possible post revolutionary brother of tomorrow. They will be two different things. In the same way that today I consider my dog "different" because it does not "speak" to me but barks. Of course I love my dog, I like him, he is useful to me, he guards me, is friendly, wags his tail; but I cannot imagine struggling for equality between the human and the canine races. All that is far beyond my imagination, is o t h e r. Tragically, this separation of languages could also be possible in the future. And, indeed, what will be supplied to the e x c l u d e d, what will make up that limited code, if not what is already becoming visible: sounds, images, colours. Nothing of that traditional code that was based on the word, on analysis and common language. Bear in mind that this traditional code was the foundation on which the illuminist and progressive analysis of the transformation of reality was made, an analysis which still today constitutes the basis of revolutionary ideology, whether authoritarian or anarchist (there is no difference as far as the point of departure is concerned). We anarchists are still tied to the progressive concept of being able to bring about change with words. But if capital cuts out the word, things will be very different. We all have experience of the fact that many young people today do not read at all. They can be reached through music and images (television, cinema, comics). But these techniques, as those more competent than myself could explain, have one notable possibility—in the hands of power—which is to reach the irrational feelings that exist inside all of us. In other words, the value of rationality as a means of persuasion and in developing self-awareness that could lead us to attack the class enemy will decline, I don't say completely, but significantly.

So, on what basis will the excluded act? (Because, of course, they will continue to act). They will act on strong irrational impulses.

Comrades, I urge you to think about certain phenomena that are already happening today, especially in Great Britain, a country which from the capitalist point of view has always been the vanguard and still holds that position today. The phenomena of spontaneous, irrational riots.

At this point we must fully understand the difference between riot and insurrection, something that many comrades do not do. A riot is a movement of people which contains strong irrational characteristics. It could start for any reason at all: because some bloke in the street gets arrested, because the police kill someone in a raid, or even because of a fight between football fans. There is no point in being afraid of this phenomenon. Do you know why we are afraid? Because we are the carriers of the ideology of progress and illuminism. Because we believe the certainties we hold are capable of guaranteeing that we are right, and that these people are irrational—even fascist—provocateurs, people whom it is necessary to keep silent at all costs.

Things are quite different. In the future there will be more and more of these situations of subversive riots that are irrational and unmotivated. I feel fear spreading among comrades in the face of this reality, a desire to go back to methods based on the values of the past and the rational capacity to clarify. But I don't believe it will be possible to carry on using such methods for very long. Certainly we will continue to bring out our papers, our books, our written analyses, but those with the linguistic means to read and understand them will be fewer in number.

What is causing this situation? A series of realities that are potentially insurrectional or objectively anything but insurrectional. And what should our task be? To continue arguing with the methods of the past? Or to try moving these spontaneous riot situations in an effective insurrectional direction capable of attacking not just the included, who remain within their Teutonic castle, but also the actual mechanism that is cutting out language. In future we shall have to work towards instruments in a revolutionary and insurrectional vein that can be read by the excluded.

Let us speak clearly. We cannot accomplish the immense task of building an alternative school capable of supplying rational instruments to people no longer able to use them. We cannot, that is, replace the work that was once done by the opposition when what it required was a common language. Now that the owners and dispensers of the capacity to rationalise have cut communication, we cannot construct an alternative. That would be identical to many illusions of the past. We can simply use the same instruments (images, sounds, etc) in such a way as to transmit concepts capable of contributing towards turning situations of riot into insurrection. This is work that we can do, that we must begin today. This is the way we intend insurrection.

Contrary to what many comrades imagine—that we belong to the eighteenth century and are obsolete—I believe that we are truly capable of establishing this slender air-bridge between the tools of the past and the dimensions of the future. Certainly it will not be easy to build. The first enemy to be defeated, that within ourselves, comes from our aversion to situations that scare us, attitudes we do not understand, and discourses that are incomprehensible to an old rationalist like myself.

Yet it is necessary to make an effort. Many comrades have called for an attack in the footsteps of the Luddites 150 years ago. Certainly to attack is always a great thing, but Luddism has seen its day. The Luddites had a common language with those who owned the machines. There was a common language between the owners of the first factories and the proletariat who refused and resisted inside them. One side ate and the other did not, but apart from this by no means negligible difference, they had a common language. Reality today is tragically different. And it will be increasingly different in the future. It will therefore be necessary to develop conditions so that these riots do not find themselves unprepared. Because, comrades, let us be clear about this, it is not true that we can only prepare ourselves psychologically; go through spiritual exercises, then present ourselves in real situations with our flags. That is impossible. The proletariat, or whatever you want to call them, the excluded who are rioting, will push us away as peculiar and suspect external visitors. Suspicious. What on earth can we have in common with those acting anonymously against the absolute uselessness of their own lives and not because of need and scarcity? With those who react even though they have colour TV at home, video, telephone and many other consumer objects; who are able to eat, yet still react? What can we say to them? Perhaps what the anarchist organisations of synthesis said in the last century? Malatesta's insurrectionalist discourse? This is what is obsolete. That kind of insurrectional argument is obsolete. We must therefore find a different way very quickly.

And a different way has first of all to be found within ourselves, through an effort to overcome the old habits inside us and our incapacity to understand the new. Be certain that Power understands this perfectly and is educating the new generations to accept submission through a series of subliminal messages. But this submission is an illusion.

When riots break out we should not be there as v i s i t o r s to a spectacular event, and because in any case, we are anarchists and the event fills us with satisfaction. We must be there as the realisers of a project that has been examined and gone into in detail beforehand.

What can this project be? That of organising with the excluded, no longer on an ideological basis, no longer through reasoning exclusively based on the old concepts of the class struggle, but on the basis of something immediate and capable of connecting with reality, with different realities. There must be areas in your own situations where tensions are being generated. Contact with these situations, if it continues on an ideological basis, will end up having you pushed out. Contact must be on a different basis, organised but different. This cannot be done by any large organisation with its traditionally illuministic or romantic claim to serve as a point of reference and synthesis in a host of different situations; it can only be done by an organisation that is agile, flexible and able to adapt. An i n f o r m a l o r g a n i s a t i o n of anarchist comrades—a specific organisation composed of comrades having an anarchist class consciousness but who recognise the limits of the old models and propose different, more flexible models instead. They must touch reality, develop a clear analysis and make it known, perhaps using the instruments of the future, not just the instruments of the past. Let us remember that the difference between the instruments of the future and of the past does not lie in putting a few extra photographs in our papers. It is not simply a matter of giving a different, more humorous or less pedantic edge to our writing, but of truly understanding what the instruments of the future are, of studying and going into them, because it is this that will make it possible to construct the insurrectional instruments of the future to put alongside the knife that our predecessors carried between their teeth. In this way the air-bridge we mentioned earlier can be built.

Informal organisation, therefore, that establishes a simple discourse presented without grand objectives, and without claiming, as many do, that every intervention must lead to social revolution, otherwise what sort of anarchists would we be? Be sure comrades, that social revolution is not just around the corner, that the road has many corners, and is very long. Agile interventions, therefore, even with limited objectives, capable of striking in anticipation the same objectives that are established by the excluded. An organisation which is capable of being "inside" the reality of the subversive riot at the moment it happens to transform it into an objectively insurrectional reality by indicating objectives, means and constructive conclusions. This is the insurrectional task. Other roads are impassable today.

Certainly, it is still possible to go along the road of the organisation of synthesis, of propaganda, anarchist educationism and debate—as we are doing just now of course—because, as we said, this is a question of a project in tendency, of attempting to understand something about a capitalist project which is in development. But, as anarchist revolutionaries, we are obliged to bear in mind this line of development and to prepare ourselves from this moment on to transform irrational situations of riot into an insurrectional and revolutionary reality.

ELEPHANT
EDITIONS
ANARCHIST
POCKETBOOKS

ELEPHANT EDITIONS

**Elephant Editions, BM Elephant, London
WCIN3XX.**

SABATE

GUERILLA EXTRAORDINARY

ANTONIO TELLEZ

Translated by Stuart Christie
Introduction by Alfredo M. Bonanno
ISBN No 1 870133 00 5
Price £2.95

This book tells of the life, the action and the death of anarchist guerilla Francisco Sabate in the struggle against Franco's dictatorship until he was killed in 1960. It shows the many ways it is possible to strike the enemy, no matter what colour of fascism it might be, rendering it of great validity still today.

STRANGE VICTORIES

THE ANTI-NUCLEAR MOVEMENT IN THE US AND EUROPE

MIDNIGHT NOTES

Introduction by Alfredo Bonanno
88 pages
ISBN No 1 870133 01 3
£1.95

An interesting analysis of the anti-nuclear movement, it looks at its composition, class analysis (lack of it), the problem of violence, opening a much-needed debate on struggle and organisation against the nuclear project seen within that of capital as a whole.

THE ANGRY BRIGADE

DOCUMENTS AND CHRONOLOGY

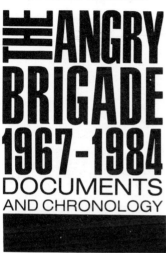

Introduction by Jean Weir
ISBN No 1 870133 02 1
60 pages
£1.20

This is a reprint of the Bratach Dubh pamphlet which is no longer available. Beginning in 1967, it shows some extent of the armed struggle carried out in Britain in the late sixties and early seventies, and reproposes the validity of the method of armed struggle against capital in all its forms.

THE CONQUEST OF BREAD

PETER KROPOTKIN

Introduction by Alfredo M. Bonanno
214 pages
ISBN No 1 870133 03 X
£3.60

One of the fundamental classics of anarchism, its present day validity lies in Kropotkin's vision of the revolutionary project as a totality, something that would be impossible if it were not already in course. Within this totality the movement finds its orientation, becomes process and project in the immense task of the class struggle between exploiter and exploited. All that would be impossible if the final dream were not really starting here and now.

ANARCHISM AND VIOLENCE

SEVERINO DI GIOVANNI

OSVALDO BAYER

Translated by Paul Sharkey
Introduction by Alfredo M. Bonanno
ISBN No 1 870133 04 8
256 pages
£3.95

Through the figure of Severino Di Giovanni and his activities in Argentina in the '20s a problem which has divided the anarchist movement from its beginning is highlighted—that of violent revolutionary action against the State. The narrative form and documented accounts, supply the reader with both a knowledge of this anarchist and the little known period in which he lived and carried on his struggle.

THE GREAT FRENCH REVOLUTION

PETER KROPOTKIN

Introduction by Alfredo M. Bonanno
Vol I pp. 1 - 304 — Vol II pp. 305 - 604
ISBN No 1870133056
3.95 per volume

Kropotkin's study of the French Revolution is a fundamental interpretation that provides us today with a number of observations of great relevance. Throughout his book Kropotkin ties his interpretation of the course of the Revolution to the continuous stream of popular action, which he sees as beginning long before the Revolution itself.

In the second volume of the Great Revolution, Kropotkin continues his interpretation of this historic event by concentrating on the clash between the Jacobins and their opponents—the Enragés and Anarchists. In this clash between authoritarians and antiauthoritarians Kropotkin draws out the origins of Marxism and Leninism within the Jacobins.